Persona

for

Faith in the Night Seasons

by

Nancy Missler

Koinonia House

Personal Application Workbook for
Faith in the Night Seasons

© Copyright 2000 by Nancy Missler

Second Printing August, 2002

Published by Koinonia House
PO Box D
Coeur d'Alene ID 83816-0347
ISBN 1-57821-101-8

All Rights Reserved. No portion of this book may be reproduced in any
form whatsoever without the written permission of the Publisher.

All Scripture quotations are from the King James Version of the Holy
Bible.

PRINTED IN THE UNITED STATES OF AMERICA

Table of Contents

Introduction

Night seasons--times of darkness, confusion and aloneness in our walk with the Lord--can do one of two things: push us *towards* God and "seeing Him always before our face" or, push us *away* from Him towards doubt, unbelief and a faith that is shipwrecked. If we can understand *what God is trying to do* by allowing a dark night and if we know *what we are to do* in order to get through it, then our faith can be strengthened and we can begin to enjoy an intimacy with God we never thought possible. Ignorance of God's basic will is at the root of many of our struggles as Christians.

It is my prayer that *Faith in the Night Seasons* might act as a road map to encourage those going through dark times that they may persevere to the incredible riches of faith and intimacy that can come as a result.

The question many ask is: Does God single out certain people for night seasons or will we all go through such times?

Personally, I don't believe God calls only certain people to this experience. I believe it's the other way around. If *we* yearn to know God intimately, and yet are not experiencing unshakeable faith in our lives nor walking by His Spirit, then *He* will allow a night season to help us along. God knows that, for most of us, a night season is the only way our spirit can be strengthened and the only way we'll learn how to enjoy intimacy with Him. If, however, we are already experiencing these things, then there is no need for a night season at all. We already are pliable to His will and we already are growing in our love-relationship with Him.

Like David, our prayer should be, "I forsaw the Lord always before my face, for He is on my right hand, *that I should not be moved.*" (Acts 2:25)

Purpose of the Workbook

The goal or purpose of this workbook is to stimulate you to apply the Scriptural principles presented in the *Faith in the Night Seasons* textbook to your life. True spiritual growth comes not from simply reading a book or attending a Bible study, but by the personal application of the material to your life.

This workbook is designed to help you learn how to have unshakeable faith in God so that you can experience *intimacy with Him* no matter what is occurring in your life. You will gain the maximum benefit from this workbook by reading a chapter in the *Faith in the Night Seasons* textbook and then completing the corresponding chapter workbook questions. You will quickly see how specific Scriptures apply to your own situation. You will receive deeper insights into God's character, His will and His great Love for you. You will also begin to understand your own *natural reactions* a little more clearly and, at the same time, learn an alternative way of dealing with them.

Jesus promises us in John 10:10 that, "[He is] come that [we] might have *life*, and that [we] might have it more abundantly." It is my prayer, through this book, to help you experience this kind of abundant Life in your soul and also to enjoy intimacy with Him in your spirit--knowing Him inside and out, the fulness of Christ.

How to Use This Workbook

This *Personal Application Workbook* is designed to accompany the *Faith in the Night Seasons* textbook. You should have your own textbook and your own workbook. Each chapter in the workbook corresponds to the same chapter in *Faith in the Night Seasons* textbook. The questions in the workbook should be completed *after* reading the corresponding chapter in the textbook.

The workbook questions are divided into three categories: **Group Discussion Questions**, **Personal Questions** and **Continue at Home Questions**.

- If you will be using this study for **personal Bible study**, it is suggested that you do all the workbook questions (Personal, Group, and At Home).

- If this study is to be used by **small discussion groups**, it is suggested that the leader of the group use the Group Discussion Questions and whatever Personal Questions are applicable. (See the *Role of the Discussion Leader* at the end of this workbook.) Continue at Home projects can be used during the week.

- Finally, if this study is to be used for a **large, corporate group** (where small discussion groups are not feasible), it is suggested that the appropriate questions be selected by the leadership and used for individual home study.

Personal Bible Study

Critical to any Bible study, whether it be personal or corporate, is prayer. Pray and ask God to search your heart and reveal anything that might hinder you from hearing Him. Then cleanse your heart of these things, so you can receive *all* that He has for you. Be sure to take advantage of the Prayer Section in the back of *Faith in the Night Seasons*. In particular, note the Inner Court Ritual on page 360.

Along with your King James Bible, it is often helpful to have the following: a modern translation of the Bible (such as the New American Standard Bible or the New King James Bible); a Bible dictionary to look up any unfamiliar words, names and places; and a concordance (Strong's Concordance comes in a paperback form).

Read the appropriate chapter in the textbook. You must understand the principles and concepts of *Faith in the Night Seasons* textbook before you can really answer the questions properly and apply the principles to your life.

Look up all the Scriptures listed under each question. Meditate upon each one. It's the Word of God that will change your life, not a textbook or a class. Write out on 3x5 cards the Scriptures that particularly minister to you. Look up the important words in the original Hebrew or Greek, using your concordance to be sure you are getting the *real* meaning of each word. So often the English translation in the Bible is far from what the original word meant.

Write out your answers in the space provided under each question. If you need more space, use the additional blank pages at the end of this workbook.

It's important to keep a personal journal. Write down all your experiences with God. Note the promises He gives you from Scripture, as well as the experiences He allows in your life. Express your real feelings and emotions about these things. Most importantly, write down the things that you give over to God as you cleanse your heart each day. (No one should ever see your journal but you.)

What a blessing and an encouragement this journal will be when you read it later on. In those times when you are going through a "night season," your entries in the journal will remind you of all that God has done for you in the past and of His complete faithfulness to perform His promises. Your journal will give you the encouragement and the *hope* to make the same faith choices again.

Group Bible Study

This workbook, along with the *Faith in the Night Seasons* textbook, can also be used for small group discussions. Learning takes place through the understanding and sharing of Biblical principles with intimate friends, such as in a small discussion group--about eight to ten people is ideal. Each of these groups should have a leader to guide the sharing. The *Role of the Discussion Leader* is explored in detail at the end of this workbook.

The first thing to do in all Bible studies is to pray. Prayer is what changes things--our hearts, our attitude, our situation and other people. Pray continually.

Always come to the study prepared, having first read the entire chapter in the textbook, then having completed the appropriate questions in the workbook.

As in the Personal Bible Study, look up all the Scriptures listed under each question and meditate upon each one. Again, it's only the Word of God that will change your life. Again, write out on 3x5 cards the Scriptures that ministered to you and look up the important words in your concordance.

Be willing to join in the discussions. If you have completed the questions and have some understanding of the chapter, you will feel comfortable in sharing. The leader of the group is not there to lecture, but to encourage others to share what they have learned.

Have your answers applicable to the chapter in discussion. Keep the discussion centered upon the principles presented in the *Faith in the Night Seasons* textbook, rather than on what you have "heard" others say or on what you have "read" elsewhere. Keep focused.

Be sensitive to the other members of the group. Listen when they speak and encourage them. This will prompt more people to share.

Do not dominate the discussion. Participate, but remember that others need to have equal time.

If you are a discussion leader, suggested answers, additional suggestions and helpful ideas are in the *Faith in the Night Seasons Leader's Guide*. Also, see the *Role of the Discussion Leader* section at the end of this workbook.

Above all, pray for God's guidance and the grace to love Him as He desires. Continue to be an open vessel to pass along His Love.

* * * * *

"*Search the Scriptures*; for in them ye think ye have eternal life: and they are they which testify of Me." (John 5:39, emphasis added)

Chapter One
My Own Night Season

Overview

Have you ever walked through a period of time where *everything* in your life was falling apart. All your hopes and dreams were being shattered and your confidence ruined. You cried out to God because you were confused and bewildered by all that was happening, and yet God seemed silent and uncommunicative.

Experiences like this have befallen many faithful, dedicated and loyal Christians throughout the ages, not because of any personal sin or rebellion, but simply because God was strengthening their faith and giving them the supernatural ability to "see" through the eyes of their spirit.

Night seasons are not just a dry time in our lives, but a Father-filtered period of time where God draws us closer to Himself. It's a time where there is no known sin in our lives, and yet God allows circumstances that darken our understanding, that negate our feelings and that put to confusion all our own plans and purposes. It's a time where He lovingly removes all of our natural and comfortable "support systems" (inside and out) so that He might replace them with total and unshakeable trust in Him. It's a time where He leads us away from depending upon "self" (our own sight and our own feelings) to depending totally upon Him. In other words, it's a time where *God teaches us by darkening us.*

Scripture tells us that God not only is light, but that He also dwells in and works through darkness. God is training us to be able to "see" through the eyes of our spirit and *not* depend upon the eyes of our own understanding or our own feelings.

If we understand what is happening to us and why God is allowing these things, then He can bring us through to a new intimacy with Him that we have never before known. If, however, we don't understand what is happening or what He is doing, then doubt and unbelief will take over and, in the end, our faith will be shipwrecked. Night seasons can either push us *towards* God and a deeper love-relationship with Him or they can push us *away* from Him into a state of unbelief, confusion and despair.

Group Discussion Questions

1) Trials can push us closer to God or farther away from Him. What is the KEY to staying in fellowship with Him during our trials?

2) Name the different areas from which trials may arise. What makes a night season any different from other trials?

3) Difficult times often reveal our true character. Why?

4) What is often at the bottom of our faith stuggles? Why is this so critical to recognize?

5) By what standard do we usually measure the validity of a promise?

6) What is God's basic will for our lives as Christians?

7) What two things must we allow God to do, in order to experience His abundant Life and enjoy intimacy with Him?

8) Explain in your own words the meaning of the "fulness of Christ."

9) What are some of the things that we often rely upon other than God?

10) Abandonment to God's will and human expectations cannot co-exist. Why not?

Personal Questions

1) Have you ever experienced a night season in your life? Were you able to stay close to God? What was the key that kept you there? Can you share your story?

2) Have you ever struggled with doubt, belief and fear? Did you follow what they were motivating you to do or did you trust God? Share.

3) Define what faith means to you. Is this the kind of faith that the Bible describes and that God desires us to have?

4) What are some of the support systems that you rely upon other than God? Be honest. Much of our healing comes when we acknowledge our self-centered ways. We all have them.

5) In your own personal walk with God, have you come to the point of being willing to relinquish all other supports in order to know Him intimately? Anything we hold on to other than God can become an idol in our life, forcing God to intervene. Write your thoughts down.

6) What do you personally think Job meant when he said, "Though You slay me, yet will I trust You"? (Job 13:15)

Continue at Home:

1) Write on a note card any Scriptures that particularly ministered to you in this chapter. Use them to help you apply these principles. Memorize them. Carry them with you or post them where you can see them as a reminder.

2) This week, talk to God about improving the quality of your daily quiet time. Schedule a specific time with Him. Listen to (and sing along with) taped worship songs for your praise time with God. Write out some of your prayers. Use a daily reading guide to help you be consistent with your Bible reading. Be accountable to someone for this time.

3) Write on a 3x5 card the steps of the Inner Court Ritual (how to give things over to God and leave them there) found on page 360 of the *Faith in the Night Seasons* textbook. Write out the steps in your own words.

Keep the cards with you--in your Bible, in your purse, in your car, etc. Believe me, you will need them.

For further study see Chapter 14 in *The Way of Agape* and Chapter 15 in *Be Ye Transformed*.

4) Begin a journal. Write down all the experiences God allows in your life this week that you need to "deal" with--situations you didn't handle properly or attitudes you developed that were not godly. *Confess* any of your thoughts or emotions that were not of faith and *repent* of them-- choose to turn around from following them. *Give those negative things to God*, and then *read His Word*. Ask Him to replace the lies with His Truth.

MEMORIZE:
Isaiah 50:10
Job 42:5
Acts 2:25

Chapter Two
Are Night Seasons Part of God's Will?

Overview

One of the reasons I wrote *Faith in the Night Seasons* is to help prevent others from suffering the confusion and the insecurity that I experienced during my own dark night season. I want others to know that they are *not* alone, that many, many other saints have experienced night seasons and lived to tell about the incredible riches that result. Night seasons *are* Scriptural and *are* God's will.

Look at Joseph's life. He endured a night season of almost 13 years! During that period of time, however, he enjoyed a wonderful intimacy with God. So much so, that others who saw him continually commented, "God must be with Him." (Genesis 39) Look at Moses's life. He endured 40 years in the wilderness, but in the end he saw God "face to face." (Deuteronomy 5:4) Look at Job's life. No one has suffered as much as Job and, yet in the end, he says, "I have heard of thee by the hearing of the ear, but now mine eye seeth thee." (42:5)

Other Scriptural examples of men who suffered night seasons are: David, Elijah, Paul and, of course, Jesus, when He said, "My God, my God, why hast thou forsaken me?" (Matthew 27:46) In more recent history, people such as Martin Luther, Charles Finney, Charles Spurgeon, Oswald Chambers, John Wesley, Watchman Nee, Francis Shaeffer, Hudson Taylor, Jesse Penn Lewis, George Fox, William Law, Catherine Marshall and many, many others have written about their own personal dark night.

Why would a loving heavenly Father put one of His faithful children through such a difficult time? Well, simply because many of us still walk by the "flesh"--our *own* feelings and the eyes of our *own* understanding. This is one of the reasons why many of us are having problems and also why our relationship with the Lord often becomes stagnant. God loves us too much, however, to allow this kind of lukewarm relationship to continue. He wants us to know Him so intimately and trust Him so completely that we won't ever be moved away from Him, even when difficulties arise in our lives. He knows that the only way we will ever have this kind of vibrant and immovable relationship is by learning to have "naked faith"--faith that rests only upon Him, not upon our feelings or our sight. Thus, He allows a Father-filtered night season into our lives hoping that this experience will push us into a deeper face-to-face relationship.

After Job's God-directed dark night, Job developed an intimacy with the Father that he had never before experienced. And the same can be true with us. By darkening our understanding, negating our feelings, confusing our thoughts and frustrating our own plans and purposes, we will be forced to depend totally upon our faith and the eyes of our spirit. This is God's will.

Group Discussion Questions

1) All Christians, at some time or another, experience problems and trials. What is a night season? How are they different from other trials? Are they Scriptural? Is Satan involved?

2) What are some of the things we can do to prepare for a night season?

3) So often we struggle against God in our night seasons. What causes us to do this? What happens if we continue to fight Him?

4) Is it true that if a believer continually surrenders his will and life to God, there need not be a night season in his life? Explain how this can be.

5) Why would a loving heavenly Father put one of His children through such a difficult time? Are these seasons truly part of His will?

6) What do you see as some of God's purposes for night seasons?

7) Where does the Bible tell us that the *kindom of God* lies? In order to experience intimacy, then, what must occur?

8) Is it possible that God "who is Light" could ever dwell in darkness? Explain.

9) Where is it (what part of our makeup) that *God* teaches us, guides us and communes with us? And where is it that *we* worship and love Him? Why is this so important to understand?

10) Why is the inward journey towards intimacy with God so very different from all the other spiritual paths that we have been on? Why do we often misunderstand His ways? Explain.

11) Why is being able to trust God in the darkness and confusion essential? What happens when we don't trust Him during these times?

12) Give some Scriptural examples of people who received a call from God, experienced some sort of success, were driven into a night season and then returned to fulfill their destiny. Briefly share their stories.

Personal Questions

1) Have you ever experienced a time in your own life where you felt totally abandoned by God? Was there any known sin in your life? Can you share your experience?

2) Real love involves trust. When you know that someone really loves and cares about you, you trust that they have your best interests at heart, even when you don't always understand what they are doing. Do you feel this way about God and His dealings with you? Are you able to trust Him unconditionally, no matter what you see or understand to be happening in your life?

3) Do you think that God singles out certain people for night seasons or do you think that we all will go through such a difficult time?

4) Do you love God enough to surrender everything to Him? What are some of the hardest things in your life to relinquish?

5) What is the number one question that God continually asks us during our night seasons? Why do we so often misunderstand this aspect of discipleship (our night seasons)?

Continue at Home:

1) Can you name some key verses in this chapter? Write them on a note cand and use them to help you apply the *Faith in the Night Seasons* principles. Carry them with you or post them where you can see them as a reminder. Memorize them.

2) Spend quiet time this week recommitting every area of your life to God. Ask God to show you any area that you are not willing to lay down to Him (you might not even be aware of them).

3) Pray and ask God to make you aware of your *sin* and *self*. In your journal, write down what He shows you. Then, confess and repent of these things and choose to relinquish them to Him.

4) Every morning, ask God to not only fill you with His Love, but also to allow that Love to be the motivation for all your choices.

READ:	**MEMORIZE:**
James 1:2 through 2:26	Romans 4:20-21
Isaiah 59:9-10	Acts 2:25
Ephesians 3:16-19	Isaiah 50:10-11
	Job 13:15

Chapter Three
God's Will and Man's Free Choice

Overview

God's basic will is to conform us into His image by teaching us how to walk in naked faith and through the eyes of our spirit. When God begins to accomplish this in our lives, we not only will begin to experience His abundant Life in our soul, but also intimacy with Him in our spirit. This is called the *fulness of Christ*. It's being filled up with God inside and out.

This transformation, however, is not automatic. There are two things that constantly stand in the way: *sin* and *self*. Thus, God must expose and strip us of these things. The name of the process that He uses to accomplish these things is *sanctification*. Sanctification is not only God's purging of our sinful acts--*the things we do*--but also His purifying of our self-centered ways--*who we are*.

How does God accomplish this sanctification in our lives? By allowing night seasons.

If we understand the above and we know what God's basic will is, then we'll have the confidence to proceed in our relationship with Him, no matter how dark and confusing our circumstances become. When we have unshakeable faith, God can bring us through to a new intimacy with Him that we have never before known. If, however, we don't understand God's will or what He is trying to do in our lives, then doubt and unbelief will consume us and, in the end, our faith will be shipwrecked.

God is working out His perfect will into the tapestry of each of our lives, and even though we might not fully comprehend all the details of what He is doing, we must have faith in His skill as the Master Craftsman. The bottom line is, "Do we trust Him?" I know in my own life, He seems to find a new way everyday to ask me that same question.

Group Discussion Questions

1) Why did God originally call us to be Christians? What was His will and purpose? Why is it so critical that we know and understand this?

2) Knowing God's will for our lives and having faith in order that He might accomplish it are inseparably linked. Why and how?

3) Name the four different aspects of God's will and give a brief explanation of each.

4) Why would God go to such lengths to redeem His fallen creation? Why is this the key to our lost identity?

5) God's basic will for the believer is for us to be conformed into His image. He accomplishes this by the process of sanctification. What exactly does this mean?

6) Does the sanctification process happen automatically? If not, why? What is it dependent upon?

7) Define "abundant Life." How does this differ from having intimacy with God? How do these two things correspond to the term "the fulness of Christ?"

8) What are the two areas that God must cleanse and purify in the sanctification process? Explain the difference between these areas? In our lifetime, is it possible to become completely sanctified body, soul and spirit? Why/ or why not?

9) Why is our free will (our choice) the most important element of our physical design? Explain.

10) We are not responsible to choose to change our negative feelings. There's no way we can do that. What then are we responsible for?

11) Where is sin birthed? Why is this so important to know and understand?

12) Our supreme purpose as Christians is not only to be conformed into Christ's image and love others, but also to love God with all our heart, mind and soul. Practically, what does this mean to you?

Personal Questions

1) What is the most important thing to remember in any trial? (Isaiah 43:2-5a; Hebrews 12:6-8; 2 Corinthians 4:17-18)

2) If in a night season we think that God has abandoned us, how can we proceed with any confidence at all?

3) God doesn't ask us to understand all that He is doing in our lives, only to believe in His Love *through* what He is doing. Do you trust God to do all that He needs to in your life in order to accomplish His perfect will? Share your heart.

Continue at Home:

1) Write on a note card the Scriptures that particularly ministered to you in this chapter. Use them to help you apply these principles. Memorize them.

2) Ask God to show you this week why knowing His basic will is so vitally important. In your journal, write the things that He reveals to you. Be prepared to share.

3) Spend quiet time with God recommitting every area of your life. If there are any areas that you are still struggling with, write these down in your journal and, by faith, give them to God.

4) Daily, ask God to fill you with His Spirit and choose to let Him be the motivation for all your choices.

READ:
Ephesians 1:9-10
John 3:16-17
1 Thessalonians 5:23
2 Thessalonians 2:13

MEMORIZE:
1 Thessalonians 4:3a
Isaiah 55:8-9
Matthew 22:37-40

Chapter Four
Knowing God's Will Personally

Overview

As we learned last chapter, there are four different aspects to God's will: His sovereign will, His revealed will, His will for mankind and His will for believers. The aspect that we are most interested in is God's will for the believer, which is sanctification. Sanctification, as mentioned before, is the process by which God conforms us into His image so that we might *outwardly* experience abundant Life and *inwardly* enjoy His presence--i.e., the fulness of Christ.

But what about daily knowing God's will for our personal lives? What about those hard everyday questions like, "Should I do...?" "Would it be better to..." "Do You want me to..." How can we know God's will for these kinds of questions? Unfortunately, human logic and reason cannot be sources of spiritual guidance here. As Christians, we cannot trust in our own understanding any more than we can trust in our own righteousness. There is a much greater scheme of things that is not yet given to our human understanding, and this plan can only be revealed spiritually.

Our ability to discern God's specific will for our lives is always affected by our love for Him. Have we obeyed Him? Are we trusting Him? Do we have faith in Him no matter what is going on in our lives? When we put Him first in our lives and unconditionally trust Him, He will always be faithful to show us His specific and personal will. Thus, there are, at least, four different ways we *can* know God's personal will for our lives: through His Word, through times of prayer and fasting, by yielding ourselves to His Spirit and by the counsel of others and our circumstances. The timing, of course, and the way that God shows us His will is always up to Him.

Group Discussion Questions

1) Is it possible to personally know God's will for our daily lives? What is the most important requirement in doing so?

2) List some of the different ways we can personally know His will. Give a short explanation of each.

3) Where is the first place we should go to get guidance from the Lord? Why is this so important?

4) What are some of the requirements to hearing God's Word clearly? What must we do personally in order to hear His Word?

5) What is a simple, but sure, barometer that assures us we *are* "in God's will"?

6) Name some of the characters in the Bible who were fortunate enough to "see" God in the midst of their harsh circumstances?

7) What is the "key" to seeing God? Why?

8) What is a good way to determine if the counseling we are getting is from God or not?

9) Name five reasons why only Jesus can be our true healer.

10) If we are in a hurry and we don't have time to pray, read Scripture, yield ourselves to God's Spirit and seek counseling, what are four important things we can do to know His will?

Personal Questions

1) Explain some of the ways we can know God's will from His Word. Can you give a personal example of a time when God directed you specifically through His Word?

2) Can we take the promises of God in the Bible literally and personally? If so, what must we do?

3) What should our response be when God asks us to wait a little longer for His promise to be fulfilled in our lives? (Romans 4:20-21; Isaiah 40:31)

4) Why is it so important to always seek God first, not His promises. Share your thoughts on this.

5) Can we determine God's will by only the circumstances in our lives? Why or why not?

Continue at Home:

1) Write on a note card all the Scriptures that particularly ministered to you in this chapter. Use them to apply the principles you are learning. Memorize them.

2) This week ask God to personally show you the times that you fall back and rely on your own ability and your own strength (the flesh), rather than depending upon His Spirit. Recognize these times and deal with these soulish things the proper way. Be sure to refer to the Prayer Journal on page 355 and, in particular, the Inner Court Ritual on page 360.

3) Every day this week, make a special time to be with the Lord. Continue to ask Him how you might improve the quality of your quiet time with Him. Continue to write out your prayer requests. Choose to give Him your expectations, your presumptions and your comparisons and ask Him to replace these things with more of His Spirit--more of His unconditional Love.

4) Note in your journal the different ways you can know God's will personally. Begin to implement these ways in your own life this week.

READ   **MEMORIZE**
James 1:1-10   Psalm 32:8
1 Corinthians 10:31   Isaiah 55:8-9
Psalm 91:14-15   John 12:24-25

Chapter Five
Why Is Faith So Important?

Overview

Faith is important because faith is the only path that leads to intimacy and the abundant Life. Faith is the only way we can walk through the darkness. Only faith enables us to set aside our own understanding, our own feelings and begin to see through the eyes of our spirit. It's the only thing that silences our emotions and calms our confusion. Thus, *faith is the key to our victory*. Without it, we will never be able to please God and Satan will always be able to devour us.

We must learn to have unshakeable faith in God no matter what is going on in our lives. This is called naked faith. It's faith that is built solely upon the Lord, not upon our emotions, our sight or our experience. Naked faith enables us to go beyond our reason and beyond our circumstances into the reality of the divine.

Many Christians, if they don't understand what God is doing through their night seasons, react the same way that I did. And, that is to fight Him the whole way. This, of course, only compounds the problem and makes everything ten times worse. The logical conclusion we come to is that God has abandoned us and that we are a total failure as a Christian. Once we begin to think this way, doubt and unbelief creep in and we end up frustrated and defeated. As we try to battle the circumstances of our lives in our own strength and our own ability, the result is that we fall away from the Lord. Thus, it's critical to understand God's basic will and to always have unshakeable faith, then it will be easier to endure the darkness and to look forward to the prize of intimacy and love that results.

If we can freely allow God to transform us in the darkness, then our faith will be strengthened and our relationship with Him perfected.

Group Discussion Questions

1) Why is having faith so important? What exactly is "naked" faith?

2) What conclusions do most people have concerning their faith in God when confronted with a night season? Why is that?

3) What is the source of real faith? (Ephesians 2:8-9) What is emotional faith and how does it survive?

4) Our faith is closely interwoven with our _____. Explain.

5) How do we build our lives upon true faith in God? What have most of us built our lives upon?

6) If faith is the ability to see everything through the eyes of our spirit, what is it that clouds and dims our sight?

7) Faith is learning to "leave ourselves in order to find ourselves." Define what this means?

8) What are some of the things that faith allows us to do?

9) How does the Bible describe *overcoming faith*? What does overcoming faith mean to you?

10) Read Chapter Six of Ephesians. Describe what the shield of faith does. Why is this shield such an important part of the armor of God that Paul exhorts us to wear?

11) What is the "work of faith" spoken of in 2 Thessalonians 1:11?

Personal Questions

1) In your own words, explain Romans 4:21, "Being fully persuaded that, what He had promised, He was able also to perform." What does this mean to you?

2) Wouldn't experiencing a night season normally turn a person away from God? Explain.

3) How can our faith possibly be "built up" in such a devastating time as a night season?

4) Have you ever personally experienced a situation where you didn't understand what God was doing or why? How did you handle it? How should you have handled it?

5) Are you building your life upon true faith in God or upon other things? Be honest.

6) We have learned that having naked faith during our night seasons is critical. Can you think of a time in your life where you experienced a difficult time, and yet you submitted to the confusion and laid still in it? (Isaiah 50:10-11) Can you share?

Continue at Home:

1) On a note card, write out all the Scriptures that particularly ministered to you in this chapter. Use them to help you apply these principles. Memorize them.

2) Ask God to show you the areas that you are *still* not willing to lay down to Him. An attitude of willingness is essential. Ask God to show you where you are falling short. Note what He reveals in your journal.

3) Every day this week, make a special time to be alone with the Lord. Ask Him to show you the areas where you are lacking in faith and the areas where you are still trusting in our own abilities. Pray that He

would teach you unshakeable faith and help you learn to walk by His Spirit in these areas. Ask Him also to help you this week to put the interests of your spouse, family and others above your own.

4) Write out on 3x5 note cards all the definitions of faith that you can find in the Bible. Pick the ones that particularly minister to you and memorize them.

READ	**MEMORIZE**
Hebrews 11	1 John 5:4
2 Corinthians 4:18	Romans 10:17
Ephesians 6	Job 13:15

Chapter Six
Faith in the Dark Night

Overview

Faith is the ability to walk "as seeing Him who is invisible," (Hebrews 11:27) no matter what is occurring in our lives. Faith is being able to say (in any circumstance), "Though He slay me, yet will I trust in Him." (Job 13:15) Faith is not seeing, not knowing, not understanding and yet, still choosing to trust God. This kind of unshakeable faith only seems to grow in times of stretching. Dark nights or night seasons are periods of time where our faith will either grow from *infancy* to *intimacy* or dwindle and die.

One of the titles of the dark night is "a night of love." This particular title fascinates me because it's so appropriate. God sends us a dark night or a night season out of *His* love for us, and the only way we can make it through this night, is by *our* love for Him. Thus, the title of "a night of Love" is, to me, perfect.

Dark nights are God-filtered periods of time where we come to know, see and love our Beloved in a way we never have before. To love God really means to become one with Him. This oneness in the spirit is where we are able to see His face always before us and are never moved away. We have become one spirit, one heart, one will and one soul with Him.

The only way this kind of a relationship can ever become a reality in our lives, however, is by unconditional faith. This is not blind faith, but simply naked faith. Naked faith is faith that rests not in something unknown, but in Someone known--in the Person of Christ. He is the One who will always be reliable, always be trustworthy and always be faithful, even though sometimes His ways are past finding out. The lesson to be learned in our dark night is that we must always walk by faith through the eyes of our spirit and not by our feelings or our sight.

Group Discussion Questions

1) Give a Scriptural definition for a dark night or a night season. Look up the Scriptures in the back of the *Faith in the Night Seasons* textbook, page 369.

2) What are some other names for the dark night? Do any of these seem to you to better describe this particular period of time? Explain how a true dark night could be called a "night of love?" What is God's goal and purpose for this "night of love?"

3) Why is it necessary that God rid us of our preoccupation with sight and feelings? What is wrong with these things?

4) What is the "key" to experiencing the kind of intimacy with God that the Bible talks about?

5) If we make the right choices, what are some of the results that can occur from a night season?

6) Is the enemy always involved in our night seasons? Is he responsible for sending the dark night? Share your views.

7) Explain what the term *suffering* really means. According to Scripture, suffering is a very important part of our growing as Christians. Why?

8) What are the two ways that we can respond to suffering?

9) Philippians 3:10 tells us that we are to be "conformed to His death." What does this mean to you? Why can't we just learn about Christ's death and suffering from what we read?

10) How can the dark night be likened to being "salted with fire"?

11) God, in His infinite Love for us, uses the way of suffering to accomplish His will. Can you give some Scriptural examples of this.

12) Explain why God needs to purge our souls of sin and self. What is He after?

Personal Questions

1) In Matthew 26:38, it says that Jesus suffered for us, leaving us an example to follow. What does this mean to you? Do you see any parallels in Jesus' life to the dark night of faith?

2) Isaiah 53:4 tells us that Jesus bore our griefs and carried our sorrows. Are there any passages in Isaiah 53 that you can personally identify with?

3) Faith that is not dependent upon our sight or our feelings means what to you? Do you personally experience this kind of faith? Explain.

4) If we already love and belong to Christ, why does He have to put us through such a difficult time as a night season? Share from your heart.

Continue at Home:

1) Write on a note card the Scriptures that particularly ministered to you in this chapter. Use them to help you apply these principles. Memorize them.

2) Over the next week, be bold enough to ask God to enable you to experience unshakeable faith in a new and deeper way.

3) As you read God's Word and look up the appropriate Scriptures this week, ask God to illuminate your heart and give you new understanding of what it means to walk by the Spirit. Since you have been more aware of making faith choices and of walking by His Spirit, have you noticed any other inner changes that have occurred in your life. God changes us from the inside out. Quite often our circumstances will not have changed much, but we will have.

4) Write out Isaiah 53:3-8. As you read these Scriptures, see if you identify with the things that Jesus suffered. Then, relinquish yourself afresh to God, being willing for Him to do whatever is necessary in your life to accomplish His will. If you are unable to do this, talk to God about your feelings and reactions.

READ	**MEMORIZE**
1 Peter 4:1; 2:21, 23	Hebrews 5:8
Philippians 2:5-9	Philippians 3:10
Matthew 26:36-39	Acts 2:25

Chapter Seven
What Is the Dark Night of the Soul?

Overview

Trials and problems come to all Christians. Trials come because of personal sin, the sins of others, the schemes of the devil and the fallen state of the human race. According to the Bible, the dark night of our soul is not just a dry time in our walk with the Lord, a period where we are having a few problems or a trial from the enemy; it's a season sent directly from God to draw us closer to Him. As He says in 1 Kings 12:24, "This thing is [sent] from Me." A true Biblical dark night is a God-sent, Father-filtered period of time where, even though there is no known sin, God allows the believer to go through feelings of darkness, confusion and aloneness.

There seems to be two aspects to the dark night, two "winters" so to speak. In the first winter, the dark night of the soul, God focuses on our *outward man* and the things that we do. During the second winter, the dark night of the spirit, He focuses on our *inward man* and all of our self-centered ways.

In the first dark night, God asks us to surrender everything in our lives that is unholy, unrighteous and not of faith. Anything that we have put first in our lives or that we rely upon other than God, He points out and desires to be re-prioritized. Even though we are positionally cleansed and sanctified by the blood of Christ when we are first born again, we will not experience God's perfection (or completion) in our lives until the sin in our lives is removed and our self-centered ways are nailed to the cross.

The dark night of the soul, therefore, is a transition time where God leads us away from depending upon ourselves to depending completely upon Him. Since we are unable to learn these lessons through our reason, our intellect or our emotions, God must teach us by darkening these areas and forcing us to rely completely upon our faith and the eyes of our spirit.

Group Discussion Questions

1) Describe the two different aspects of the dark night. In the second night, why must God remove all other supports?

2) A perfect analogy for the two night seasons is like a gardener pruning his trees. In the first night, the gardener only prunes the tree's branches. But in the second night, according to this analogy, what does he do? Explain.

3) The dark night is not just a dry time in our walk, a trial from the enemy or a period where we are having a few problems, it's_ _____ ____ _____ ____ ___ _ ____ _ _____. (1 Kings 12:24)

4) The "answer" (the solutions) to the first dark night is what? What, then, is the answer (or the solution) to the second dark night?

5) What exactly is our soul? When we become *born again* what happens to our soul?

6) What is the "flesh?" What is the only way that we can be freed from the flesh's influence?

7) There is only one way that God can strengthen our spirit. What is it? When He begins to do this, what happens to us if we don't understand what He is doing?

8) God has many goals and purposes for the dark night of the soul. What are some of them? What are some of the benefits?

9) Who does the dark night of the soul happen to? Give several categories of people.

10) God is the One who sends the dark night and God is the One who will get us out. How does He do this?

11) What is it that makes a "great" Christian? Define it.

12) The Bible tells us we are to be "perfect." (James 1:4) How does this occur? Is this something that we can experience here on earth?

Personal Questions

1) Explain in your own words some of the things God is looking for in each of our lives as Christians?

2) How would you personally describe what loving God means?

3) What matters more to you in your life than anything else?

4) What are some of the questions that you personally ask God when you are in a hard place which really only compounds the problems? What are some more appropriate questions you might ask Him?

5) How do you react when everything that you planned for, desired and hoped for blows up in your face? How does God want you to react?

6) Why are your reactions to a night season so critical?

7) How do your friends and family see you during difficult times?

8) If you find yourself in a night season, what is the most important thing you can do?

9) In your own words, why is doubt so sinister? Can you describe the three primary sources of doubt that we covered in this chapter? Have you seen these in your own walk with God?

Continue at Home:

1) Write on a note card the Scriptures that particularly ministered to you in this chapter. Use them to help you apply these principles.

2) Take a good, honest look at your life. Ask God to show you the areas where you lack faith. Half of the battle is recognizing what is really going on *inside* of you. Once you understand what the problem is, then you can choose, by faith, to give that area over to God. It's so much easier to ask God to point these things out now than for Him to take matters into His own hands because He loves you.

3) The reality of denying ourselves--surrendering ourselves--is a painful and difficult task. It's impossible to do this, apart from Christ work in us. Our responsibility is only to be willing. He, then, will be free to accomplish the job through us. This week, ask God to show you the areas that you are still "not willing" to hand over to Him. Note these in your journal. Pray about them and by faith, give them to God.

4) Note this week your reactions to hard situations. Our reactions determine our walk. Ask God to make you more aware of your responses. Note in your journal what happens. Try to learn from your mistakes.

READ	MEMORIZE
Mark 14:32-36	Mark 14:36b
Psalm 42	John 12:25
2 Corinthians 4:8-11	Psalm 112:4

Chapter Eight
Passing Through the Night

Overview

The dark night of the soul is a time where God darkens our understanding, negates our feelings and puts to confusion our own plans and purposes. It's a time where our confidence is shattered, our personal hopes ruined and we become filled with doubt and unbelief. As a result, we feel like giving up and running away. It's as if God has completely abandoned us.

The only way we will ever make it through this period of time is by learning to walk in unshakeable faith. This kind of faith silences our emotions and integrates our knowing and our unknowing and affects everything we do. It's the *key* to our victory.

Scripture tells us that, by faith, we must submit to the confusion, stand still in it and trust God anyway. As Isaiah 50:10 says, "[We are to] trust in the name of the Lord, and stay upon [our] God."

But, how do we do this practically?

First of all, we must stop asking God "why?" As Job found, God is the Potter and we are just the clay. The Potter doesn't have to tell the clay what He is doing. The clay must simply have faith and trust in the Potter's love and master craftsmanship. In the same way, we must continue to hope and rest in God's promises, regardless of how we feel, what we think or what our circumstances are. Next, we must cease doubting, guard against discouragement and stop blaming others. Finally, we must, by faith, rejoice in His word and praise His name in all things. It's imperative to remain completely abandoned to His will, regardless of what we see to be happening. Job gave us a perfect example to follow when he said, "Though He slay me, yet will I trust in Him." (Job 13:15)

Group Discussion Questions

1) If we find ourselves in a night season, what are some of the things that we should do? Why is praising God at all times so very important?

2) During a dark night, what are some of the things we "feel?" Why is it important to express our feelings to God and deal with them? Why is it so important that we not become discouraged.

3) Why is this period of time dangerous for us? When we don't understand what God is doing, why are our problems magnified?

4) Others have walked through night seasons and lived to tell about it. Why is it so important for us to know this?

5) What are some of the Scriptural analogies that God has laid out to help us understand night seasons? Describe each one.

6) In order to experience oneness with God, what must *He* do?

7) In order to enter the Holy Place of God's presence, we must not only present our bodies as a living sacrifice on the Brazen Altar, but we must also _____ __ __ ____.

8) Why is it so critical that we cooperate with God in this breaking process?

Personal Questions

1) Why do you think it's so important to deal with our *sin* and *self* and to continually give things over to God? During a night season, what happens if we become consumed in our negative thoughts and emotions? How can we proceed with any confidence?

2) When you were going through hard times, have you ever had remarks from your friends or your family like "What's wrong with you?" "Come on, get on with your life!" How did you handle those remarks? How would God have wanted you to handle their response.

3) What do you think the Lord means in Isaiah 50:10 when He exhorts us to "stay upon God"? Is this really possible in a night season? How? What are we actually doing?

4) If we don't stand still and stay upon God, what does Isaiah say will happen? (Isaiah 5:11,"walking in the light of your own fire") What does this actually mean?

5) What is one of the most effective and yet very practical ways of standing still in the storm and surrendering our lives to God?

6) We must never harbor any bitterness or resentment against those involved in our trials. Who is the One that will revenge us? How does He do this? Has He done this for you?

7) The less we struggle against God, the less the trial will hurt. Why is this true? Has this been the case in your own life? Share

8) Should we pray for relief from our trial? What do we pray for?

9) Does God reveal His plans and purposes as we are going through our night season, or does He just let us go through it in blind faith?

10) What is the only way we can get through a difficult time like this? Why is it so important that we catch our first negative thoughts?

Continue at Home:

1) Write down the Scriptures that particularly ministered to you in this chapter. Use them to help you apply these principles. Memorize them. Carry these cards with you or post them where you can see them as a reminder.

2) This week, write out on a 3x5 card some of the things you might "do," should you ever experience a night season. Be prepared ahead of time with a godly mind-set so that your reactions during the trial will please the Lord.

3) Ask God to show you this week the times that you trust in your own abilities and strengths and not His. Recognize these times and deal with them. Go through the Inner Court Ritual. Ask Him to show you how to simply rest and hope in His promises. Keep a record in your journal of any new insights that He gives you.

4) Again, make a special time to be with the Lord this week. By faith, choose to give Him the sin and self that He exposes and ask Him to reveal even the hidden things. Note your victories in your journal.

READ	**MEMORIZE**
2 Corinthians 1:3-5	Hebrews 13:5b
Malachi 3:3-4	Isaiah 61:3a
1 Peter 1:7-9	Ephesians 5:2
Psalm 18	Philippians 4:4, 6-7

C

Chapter Nine
Our Human Spirit

Overview

All communication with God occurs in the spirit. Man's spirit was once the head over the whole man, including his soul. But because of Adam's fall, the soul and spirit became intermingled, with the soul becoming the dominant force. Thus, all communication with God came to a stop. Man's spirit simply became a resident or a prisoner of his soul.

Consequently, when we are born into the human race, like Adam, our spirit is dead and our soul is naturally the predominant force, controlling all that we do. Thus, in order to once again commune and fellowship with God, we must be "born again" and receive a new spirit (God's Spirit). God's Spirit uses our human spirit like a carrier or a transport to restore spiritual communication.

Once we are born again, our spirit becomes the place in us where God dwells and also the place where He meets with us. When our spirit is cleansed and purified, we are able to see, hear and communicate with Him clearly. When there is sin and self-centeredness in our lives, not only is our soul contaminated, but our spirit is also defiled and our fellowship with God is hindered. Thus, one of the things that God is teaching us through the sanctification process is how to allow our spirit to direct our lives, not our soul. In other words, the process of sanctification is simply the process of restoring our spirit to its rightful place as director of our souls.

Our biggest difficulty, then, as Christians is that our spirit must be untangled from our soul in order to break free from its influence and rule. The true spiritual man is one in whom the spirit rules, not the soul. Therefore, real advancement in our Christian walk can only be measured by the growth of our spirit.

Group Discussion Questions

1) Can you describe how our soul and spirit first became intermingled-- with our soul being the dominant force?

2) What is it that defiles our spirit? What is the result? Because of the defilement of our spirit, what is our greatest problem as Christians? (Hebrews 4:12)

3) In practical terms, what does it mean when we say that the "spirit has been quenched"? Where does communication with God always occur?

4) What is the basic principle that God is trying to teach us through our night seasons?

5) Our defiled soul is the biggest hindrance to our being able to walk by the spirit. What is the remedy to this?

6) Define what our spirit is? What is a good analogy that helps in the explanation?

7) Our body is conscious of what two things? Our soul is conscious of what one thing? Our spirit is conscious of what?

8) What happens to our spirit when we are "born again"?

9) Briefly define and describe the three functions of our spirit?

10) What is the one thing, above everything else, that determines our growth in the Lord?

11) Describe what sanctification really is. What are the two things that God constantly highlights in us?

Personal Questions

1) In your own words, describe what your conscience is. Give examples of how your conscience works in your own life.

2) Describe what your intuition is. Again, give examples from your own life.

3) How is the third function of our spirit, our communion and fellowship with God, any different from the other two functions of our spirit?

4) In your own words, explain, the difference between your spirit and your soul. Has it helped in your personal walk with the Lord to distinguish their differences? Share how.

5) Our conscience is what gives us that "peace that passes all understanding." Peace is a good barometer to ascertain if we have a cleansed conscience or not. Describe how this works in your life. Give examples.

6) Must we wait until all sin and self has been dealt with in order to enjoy God's presence? Explain how this works in your life.

7) Why do you personally think communion and fellowship, the third function of the spirit, is so important? Share from your own experience.

8) Does being able to preach a good sermon, having an extensive knowledge of the Bible and possessing many spiritual gifts qualify one as being mature? Explain.

Continue at Home:

1) Write on a note card all the Scriptures that ministered to you in this chapter. Use them to help you apply these principles. Memorize them.

2) Ask God this week to make you aware of your choices. Ask Him to remind you when you should be making faith choices. Note the times you hear Him and you obey. Note also the times you disregarded His promptings.

3) Conduct an experiment: Watch for incidents in your life where your conscience directs you to do something. Note in your journal how you reacted. Also, be aware of the times you choose not to follow what your conscience is telling you. When you recognize this (even if it is days later), stop, pray, identify the problem, confess it, repent of it, give it to God and then get into His Word. Be prepared to share the results of your experiment.

READ	**MEMORIZE**
Romans 8:16-17	1 John 5:12
Acts 2:38	Hebrews 4:12
1 Thessalonians 5:23	Isaiah 24:15

Chapter Ten
What Is the Dark Night of the Spirit?

Overview

As mentioned before, there seems to be two aspects to the dark night. The dark night of the soul is the time where God focuses on our *outward man* (the things that we do); whereas, the dark night of the spirit is where God focuses on our *inward man* (who we are). In other words, in the second night, God exposes our human nature itself. He brings to light our "root systems"--all our preconceived belief systems, our secret habits, our hidden motives and all of our other self-centered ways. He exposes these things not to defeat us, but so that we will see these things and choose to crucify them.

Quite often we are hindered from a life of freedom in the Spirit, because of what we think and perceive down deep. Much of what we *do* is based upon our own pre-conceived (and sometimes erroneous) beliefs. These belief systems not only undergird and support our every thought and feeling, they also influence our actions. If we want to change our behavior, we must first discover what untruths we are believing. Once these are exposed and dealt with, our behavior will also have a chance to change.

Therefore, it's not necessarily our sinful actions that God focuses on in the second dark night, as much as it is our own human nature--our natural self-orientation, self-reliance and self-love. These are attitudes that do not reflect Him and, thus, He wants these things eliminated from our lives.

God desires to lead us away from depending upon self and what we think, feel and see to where we have an unshakeable faith and trust in Him. Through this sanctification process we will come to know Jesus as we never have before and experience an intimacy with Him that we never thought possible. Some other results of this dark time are: a deeper compassion for others, a peace that passes all understanding and learning to worship Him in Spirit and truth. By learning to walk through our night seasons in faith, we will surely glorify Him in all that we do.

Group Discussion Questions

1) How does the dark night of the spirit differ from the dark night of the soul?

2) In order to fellowship with the Lord in the Holy Place of our hearts, what two things must be dealt with on a regular basis?

3) In your own words, what is *naked faith*? What does the night of the spirit have to do with naked faith?

4) The foundation of everything spiritual is the cross. Explain how the cross and abundant Life are connected.

5) What is the difference between the cross that cleanses us from sin and the cross that deals with our self?

6) What is the difference between soulish purification and spiritual purification? What is it that portrays an unpurified spirit?

7) If we insist upon "feeling" God's presence, why will it be impossible to make it through our dark night? The feeling of being abandoned by God is one of the most devastating experiences of all? Why?

8) What is the difference between *abandonment to God's will* and just plain *apathy*?

9) What are some of God's goals and purposes for the dark night of the spirit?

10) Why is it so important to relinquish our children and our babies to God? What is at stake?

11) Name some of the benefits of the dark night of the spirit?

12) Why would God allow the enemy to give us false visions and false prophecies? How can we be aware of this and not fall for his tactics?

Personal Questions

1) Give some examples of self-centered ways in your own life? How do these things rule you without you even being aware of it?

2) In your own words, what does it mean to have a "pure spirit"? How does our spirit get polluted? Give examples in your own life.

3) What are some thoughts and emotions we might experience during a dark night? Can you personally relate to any of these?

4) What do you think the term "disappointed hope" really means? Have you ever personally experienced this? Share.

5) If you ever find yourself in a dark night of the spirit, what are some things you can do to get through it?

6) Why is it dangerous to put expectations on friends and family during our night seasons? Have you ever personally experienced someone close to you letting you down in a very critical time in your life? What did you do? What would be the best way to handle this situation?

7) In your relationship with God, do you find yourself depending upon your feelings and your own understanding? What can you do in the future to change this to become naked faith?

Continue at Home:

1) Write on a note card all the Scriptures that ministered to you in this chapter. Use them to help you apply these principles. Memorize them.

2) Ask God this week to show you all the areas, all the things and all the people that you depend upon other than Him. One by one, choose to give these things over and to depend upon Him alone. Note in your journal what He shows you and what you choose to relinquish.

3) Ask God to make you aware of your choices this week. Ask Him to remind you when you should be making faith choices rather than feeling or sight choices.

4) In Matthew 26:39, Jesus says, "Not as I will, but as Thou wilt." Note the times this week that you had to apply this Scripture to your life. Did you recognize your self-centered ways immediately? Were you able to give them over to God right away? Was He faithful to change your feelings to match your faith choice? Be prepared to share.

READ	**MEMORIZE**
Philippians 2:5-8	Philippians 3:10
2 Corinthians 7:1	Job 13:15
Matthew 27:33-50	Hebrews 11:27
Psalm 77	1 Chronicles 28:20
Mark 15:33-34	

Chapter Eleven
Dwelling in His Presence

Overview

During a night season, it's almost impossible for us to remain neutral or impartial. Dark nights will do one of two things: either we will end up more in love with Jesus and "seeing Him always before our face" or, we will end up falling away from Him full of doubt and unbelief with our faith shipwrecked.

If we can begin to see that night seasons *are* Biblical, begin to understand what God's purposes are in them and learn how to walk in faith through them, then this period of time can end up pushing us towards an intimacy with God that we have never before known. Night seasons are simply the bridge over which our faith must travel on the road to intimacy.

Intimacy with God does not mean we must turn our backs on the world, seclude ourselves and seek only spiritual things. Intimacy with God simply means living the reality of this life, but at the same time, having an all-pervasive awareness of His presence. It means experiencing His nearness, His guidance, His revelations, His anointing, His Love, His Power, His peace and His joy, even during our daily events. It means constantly fellowshiping and communing with Him in the spirit, hearing His still small voice, receiving His supernatural discernment of things and knowing He will never leave us or forsake us, even as we go about our daily routine.

The thing we must always keep in mind is that only God can bring this intimacy about. We are able to enjoy His presence only to the degree that we have become holy and allowed Him to cut away *sin* and *self*. Anything less than holiness cannot stand in His presence. Thus, we must continually allow Him to highlight the areas that need to be surrendered so that we can continue to enjoy more and more fellowship with Him.

Group Discussion Questions

1) Why did the Messiah come in the first place? What was His purpose?

2) What does the word *mysticism* really mean? What is Christian mysticism? Does this mean visions, voices and dreams? Why or why not?

3) Define intimacy. Is this kind of fellowship with God really possible? Give some Scriptures as a reference.

4) Where does intimacy with God occur? Why does this kind of intimacy seem so difficult and so elusive for many of us? Explain.

5) What does intimacy with God result from? What is it that prevents it?

6) How does the dark night of the spirit fit into the process of intimacy with God? Who brings this kind of intimacy about? What exactly happens?

7) Why was the Altar of Incense in Solomon's Temple so important? What does it represent?

8) In Scripture, what does the verb *agapao* mean?

9) God uses the word "perfection" throughout Scripture. What does He mean by this? As humans, can we ever reach a state of perfection?

10) According to Scripture there are two ways we can "know" God. Define each way and share what the differences are.

Personal Questions

1) Has the analogy of the Inner Court Ritual in Solomon's Temple--where the priests carried the hot coals from the Brazen Altar in the Inner Court to the Incense Altar in the Holy Place--helped you to understand the process of intimacy? Explain.

2) In your own words, explain simply what you believe God is doing during the dark night of the spirit.

3) Describe why you believe God uses the marriage and the marriage act throughout Scripture to represent His most intimate truths. Give some Scriptural examples.

4) Do you personally have trouble being intimate with the Lord? What do you think is the problem?

5) What are some simple guidelines to follow in order to abide in God's presence? Have these been helpful in your own life?

Continue at Home:

1)Write on a note card the Scriptures that particularly ministered to you in this chapter. Use them to help you apply these principles. Memorize them and place them where you can easily see them as a constant reminder.

2) Take a good, honest look at your life. Ask yourself, "do I really have intimacy with God? Do I experience His presence, His guidance, His Love and Power in the way that the Bible talks about?" If you don't, ask yourself, "What am I going to do about it?" Hosea 4:16 talks about how people will go into bondage if they don't have intimate knowledge of God. Are you going to settle for that? Talk to Jesus about it. Pray about it. Let your answer change your life.

3) Continually be aware of the self-centered things that take away your peace and that prevent intimacy with God. Confess them, repent of them and then give them to God. Note your progress in your journal.

4) This week, especially, watch over your heart and let His Spirit (in your heart) be the motivation for all you choose to do.

READ	**MEMORIZE**
Psalm 140:13	Psalm 24:3-4
Hebrews 10:19, 22-23	Galatians 2:20
John 17:20-24	Ephesians 3:19
Ephesians 3:14-19	Colossians 3:11
	Psalm 16:11
	Acts 2:25

Chapter Twelve
Results of Intimacy

Overview

Our spirit can only be released according to the degree of brokenness in our lives. When we speak of brokenness, we simply mean the breaking of our soulish powers. Consequently, the more our soul can be broken, the more God can release our spirit and the more sensitive we can become, not only to Him, but also to others. Unless we have been broken and our spirit released, not only will our communication with God be quenched, but also our spiritual fellowship with others will be hindered. Unless we share spirit to spirit, others will not be able to hear or see Jesus though us. In other words, without being led by God's Spirit, we will not be able to really touch the heart of another person.

Because loving others as ourselves is God's commandment, He allows circumstances into our lives that will bring about the breaking of our outward man so that our spirit may be released and others touched. Our soul and spirit must be separated not only so that we can minister to others, but also so that nothing on the outside of us will affect, move or disturb our intimacy with Him on the inside. Once our spirit has been released, God can then pour out His Spirit upon us and we can be filled with the fulness of God. In other words, we'll be filled inside and out with His Spirit of Love.

Night seasons, therefore, are designed by God not only to bring about the above things, but also to draw us into an intimacy with Him that we have never before known. God does it all. He is the One who brings this union about. First, He quickens our spirit; then He purifies, renews and strengthens it. (To have a renewed spirit means that our conscience has become cleansed, our intuition heightened and our communion sweetened.) Finally, He fills us and empowers us by His Spirit, at which point, we can truly serve God with our spirit and love others as He desires.

Group Discussion Questions

1) Can you name and define the variety of ways that the Holy Spirit uses to draw us to Himself (through our spirit)?

2) Our spirit can only be released according to the degree of
_____ in our lives. Why is this true?

3) What does it mean to have a clear conscience? Define and explain.

4) The second function of our spirit is our intuition. What is its function?

5) Describe what the third function of our spirit is and why it's so unique.

6) Give some Scriptural examples of people who had wonderful
communion or friendship with God.

7) God's Word works alongside ___ _____ to give us His _____
_____.

8) What has to occur before our spirit can be released from our inner man. Why is this so important?

9) Once our spirit has been released, God's *dumamis* power can then be employed. What does this actually mean?

10) God says that we are to worship Him in the beauty of holiness. What does this mean? Whose holiness is it? Give Scriptures. Where does this holiness come from?

Personal Questions

1) In your own words, how can a night season lead to intimacy with God? Have you ever experienced this? How can we stay in this kind of intimate fellowship, especially if our night season continues?

2) Wouldn't a night season experience like this turn a person away from God? How can we bring glory to God after such a difficult time?

3) In your own words, what does a strengthened spirit mean? Is this something that you have experienced? Share.

4) What does brokenness mean to you and why do you think God not only allows it, but desires it?

5) Has it been helpful to you being able to see and visualize what happened in Solomon's Temple and how it was filled with God's Spirit from the inside out? Explain.

6) Why do you think the power of the Spirit is often the first power we experience after we are born again, but often the last power we come to understand?

7) Define what worshiping God "in spirit and truth" means to you? (John 4:23)

Continue at Home:

1) Write on a note card all the Scriptures that ministered to you in this chapter. Use them to help you apply these principles. Memorize them.

2) Write out Acts 2:25. Ask yourself, "Am I really willing to walk in an intimate, face-to-face, relationship with God no matter how I feel, what I think, how others treat me or what my circumstances are?" "Am I really willing to allow God to do whatever He deems necessary in my life so that *nothing* will move me away from His presence?" If you find yourself not willing, then ask yourself why. Are you afraid? Be honest. Ask Jesus to reveal the true reason and then, by faith, work it through. Go through the Inner Court Ritual.

3) This week see how long you can remain in the presence of Jesus. The big task is not only experiencing His presence, but the ability to actually

remain there. Remaining in God's presence is not sequestering yourself in your home and never leaving your prayer closet, but simply having an all-pervasive awareness of His presence wherever you go. Note what occurs in your journal. Be prepared to share.

READ	**MEMORIZE**
1 Corinthians 2:10-12	John 12:24-25
John 15:13-16	Ephesians 5:18b
2 Corinthians 7:1	2 Corinthians 12:9

Chapter Thirteen
Further Blessing from Intimacy

Overview

Intimacy with God offers us more benefits than we could ever possibly mention. Some of the blessings are: continually seeing God's presence through the eyes of our spirit; knowing He hears us and answers our prayers; experiencing His fruitfulness in our lives and knowing His joy, His contentment, His peace and His rest. It's interesting because joy, peace and faith all are inter-linked. Joy comes from knowing the presence of the Lord; peace comes from being fully persuaded that God will do as He promised; and, faith comes from seeing Him in all things.

Some further benefits of intimacy with God are: hating sin, receiving His Love in a new and powerful way and discerning His thoughts. Intimacy also brings us a desire to share the gospel with others. Christ has become our life and thus, it's very natural to share what He is doing in our lives. God doesn't just want a *revelation* of Christ in our lives, He wants a *reproduction* of Christ in our lives. When we are conformed into His image we *will* reflect him in all that we do. The proof of our being transformed, however, is shown by what we *do*.

Intimacy with God is the capstone or the pinnacle of our journey with Him. Intimacy is the meaning and purpose of our lives. Again, the big question is: How do we stay in the presence of God? It's one thing to experience God's presence, but it's quite another to be able to stay there. How can we do that? Immovable intimacy is accomplished by remaining abandoned to God's will, no matter what happens in our lives. This is the whole secret to the Christian walk--detachment from sin and self and remaining abandoned to God's will. This means leaving the success or failure of *all* issues with God.

As we learn to walk in naked faith through the good times as well as the bad, we will begin to experience the ability to remain in God's presence. David gave us his example, "I foresaw the Lord always before my face; for He is on my right hand, *that I should not be moved*." (Acts 2:25)

Group Discussion Questions

1) Name some of the blessings that can result from intimacy.

2) How does Scripture tell us we can obtain the joy of the Lord? Quote appropriate Scriptures.

3) Read 2 Corinthians 4:8-9 and explain what Paul is talking about here?

4) Contentment leads to the rest of God or "the promised land" that the Old Testament talks about. What does this really mean and what is the key to this kind of rest?

5) Intimacy with Jesus not only gives us freedom from guilt, but also freedom from _____,_____ and _____. Freedom from guilt means what?

6) Intimacy with God affords us not only freedom from guilt, but also freedom from our enemies. How does this work? How is this shown forth in Solomon's Temple?

7) The essence of pride is "I will" and God hates pride. Describe what true humility is and why it's so important. What is the only way to humility?

8) It's difficult enough to reach intimacy with God. What is the secret to staying there?

9) The whole secret of the Christian walk is detachment from sin and self and abandonment to God's will. What are some practical ways we can remain abandoned to God?

10) What is the biggest obstacle to this kind of abandonment?

11) Give some Scriptural examples of total submission and abandonment to God's will.

12) Describe the difference between abandonment to God's will and passivity.

Personal Questions

1) The proof of our being like Christ is shown how? By our words? By our church attendance? By our prayers? By what? Explain.

2) Is contentment determined by our circumstances and our feelings? If not, what is contentment the result of? Give personal examples.

3) We have the continual choice to dwell with God at the Incense Altar of our hearts or dwell in our circumstances. Where do you focus most of your time? Be honest.

4) In your own words, what does being an *overcomer* mean? Are you an overcomer in your own life?

5) Brother Lawrence wrote a book called "Practicing the Presence of Jesus." In it, he describes the importance of living for the moment. What does this mean to you? Do you do this?

6) Throughout this study we have talked about "unshakeable faith." Do you have this kind of faith? Do you see a difference in your faith-relationship with God since you began this study? Has it helped?

Continue at Home:

1) Write on a note card all the Scriptures that ministered to you in the chapter. Use them to help you apply these principles. Memorize them. Again, post them where you can see them so they can constantly remind you of these principles.

2) Be bold enough this week to ask God to expose the soulish things in your life. Ask Him to separate them from the spiritual. Don't be overwhelmed when He does. Use the Inner Court Ritual to deal with the things that He brings us. Everything He exposes, and that you are faithful to deal with, allows you to enjoy His presence even more.

3) Philippians 2:13 tells us that God is in us not only "to will," but also "to do." This week, continually pray for God's power to produce His Life in you. Share situations that He gives you to practice this.

4) Note the fruit of the Spirit that you see in your life this week. Are your reactions any different than when you began this study? Are you able to maintain intimacy with God even in the middle of difficult situations? Is that any different than it was before? Do you see any other changes occurring in your inner man? Note them in your journal and share them with the class if you so desire.

READ
2 Corinthians 6:3-10
Deuteronomy 6:10-11

MEMORIZE
Acts 2:25
1 Timothy 1:5
Philippians 4:11b

Chapter Fourteen
My Own Love Affair with Jesus

Overview

As we close our exploration of how to have *faith in the night seasons*, it's appropriate to remember the example that God gives us in the Bible. Throughout the Scriptures, God uses the eagle as a perfect example of the freedom that is available to us during our storms, if we keep our eyes focused directly on Him.

Nature books tells us that the eagle is one of the only birds that has a special third-eye lens that enables him to look at and fly directly towards the sun, even during a storm. The eagle is born with the basic instinct to know when a storm is approaching, and when it does, to spread out his wings and allow the wind to pick him up and lift him high *above* the storm. By doing this, he is freed from the effects of the storm and his enemies are unable to follow him. Now, he hasn't escaped the storm, but has used it to lift him higher.

The same thing is possible with us. We all have storms in our lives, but if we know how to keep our eyes focused on the Lord and let the storm bring us closer to Him, then we, too, will be able to soar above our problems and our enemies, just like the eagle. *The storms of life will not have overpowered us, but actually empowered us into the presence of Jesus.*

Group Discussion Questions

1) Psalm 30:5 tells that that "Weeping may endure for a night, but joy cometh in the morning." What do you believe that the psalmist is talking about here?

2) The only way we can continually relinquish our lives to God is by knowing that He loves us. We can't lay our lives down to someone we don't think loves us. Do you personally know that God loves you?

3) Can a Christian stay in a perfect experiential union with God--seeing Him at all times? Why or why not? What is the secret to staying in His presence?

4) Do you now understand, a little more clearly, what being filled with *the fulness of Christ* is? (Ephesians 3:14-19) What is your definition of this? What two things must occur for this to happen?

5) Describe what you believe Job meant when he says "I have heard of thee by the hearing of the ear: but now mine eye seeth thee." (Job 42:5)

Personal Questions

1) As a result of this study, when storms hit your home now, are you able to keep your eyes more and more focused on Jesus? Give examples.

2) Over the last few months, do you recall a time or an incident where the Lord seemed particularly close and you truly sensed His presence? Can you describe the incident and what you had done?

3) A "kindled soul" is one who desires, above everything else, to be *one* with God. The log is finally consumed and united with the fire. Do you desire intimacy with God so much that you trust Him to do whatever is necessary to bring it about? If not, what do you see as the obstacle?

4) In your everyday experience, do you have the assurance that Jesus will *never* leave or forsake you? Share your thoughts and feelings.

5) The Song of Solomon says, "I am my beloved's, and his desire is towards me." (7:10) Are you Jesus' beloved? Do you know that His desire *is* towards you? Write this Scripture out on a 3x5 card and post it where you can always see it. Choose to believe, by faith, what God says.

Continue for the Rest of Your Life

1) Don't put this study on a shelf and forget it. Continually keep *Faith in the Night Seasons* foremost in your mind. Keep reading the book over and over again and make the Prayer Journal a daily routine. Constantly make faith choices to walk by the Spirit so that you can stay an open channel, not only receiving and passing on God's Life, but also enjoying intimacy with Him--i.e., the fulness of Christ.

2) Ask God to continue to show you the areas in your life where you are not walking in naked faith. As He reveals these areas to you, go through the steps in the Inner Court Ritual. Stay that cleansed and open vessel before Him in Love.

3) Continue to practice the Inner Court Ritual daily. Keep your cards with those four steps close at hand. So many have their lives changed as a result of learning these principles of God, but once the study is over, they go back to their old habits and their old ways. Don't let that happen to you. Continue for the rest of your life to be led by the Spirit and to enjoy intimacy with God by having *Faith in the Night Seasons*.

4) Keep your precious quiet time before the Lord. Read His Word daily. Let Him continue to cleanse, change and transform you into His image.

5) Continue your journal. It's a wonderful way of documenting your spiritual adventure with God and of being able to review all that He has done for you.

"I foresaw the Lord always before my face; for He is on my right hand, *that I should not be moved.*" (Acts 2:25)

Role of the Discussion Leader

Your role as a leader is simply to stimulate discussion by asking the appropriate questions and encouraging people to respond.

Your leadership is a gift to the other members of the group. Keep in mind that they, too, share responsibility for the group. If you are nervous, realize you are not the first to feel this way. Many Biblical leaders--Moses, Joshua and even the apostle Paul--felt nervous and inadequate to lead others.

Leader Objectives

The following are suggested objectives to help you become an effective leader.

- To guide the discussion, to clarify understanding and to keep the group focused on the lesson.

- To steer the group into a meaningful exchange among themselves.

- To help the participants learn from each other.

- To be a neutral person leading the discussion back to Scripture and the key points if it wanders.

- To assist the group in finding practical applications for the principles discussed.

- To encourage each person to participate in the group discussion.

- To make the discussion group a non-threatening place for all to share their ideas.

- To have a positive attitude and to provide encouragement to the group.

- To guide, rather than dominate, the discussion.

Preparing to Lead

First of all, it's critical that you, the leader of the discussion group, be a cleansed vessel filled with God's Love and Wisdom--a "living example" of someone who is being conformed into Christ's image. This message must first be applied to your own life. Otherwise, you will not be genuinely prepared to lead others. You must have a working knowledge of the *Faith in the Night Seasons* principles, so you can share what God has done in your own life. You cannot "give out" something you have never "experienced" for yourself.

Only by being real and transparent yourself, sharing your own failures as well as your victories, will genuineness ever be brought into the discussion. It's important to remember that *you don't have to be "perfect" in order to guide a discussion, you simply must be an open vessel pointing others to the only One who is perfect--and that's Jesus.*

Paramount to any Bible study is prayer. Be sure to pray for the group before and after each study and do much private prayer during the discussion itself. Pray for each member of the group during the week, always remembering that prayer is the only thing that unleashes the power of God to work in all our lives.

Read the assigned chapter in the *Faith in the Night Seasons* textbook. Answer each question in the corresponding chapter in the workbook. Meditate and reflect upon each passage of Scripture as you formulate your answers.

You might also want to purchase the *Faith in the Night Seasons Leader's Guide* containing "suggested" answers for each question. There are no "right" answers; these are just suggestions. Be sure to allow the Holy Spirit room to answer the questions the way He desires.

As a leader, you must be a sensitive listener, not only to the members of the group but also to the Holy Spirit. As you ask the appropriate questions, allow the Holy Spirit to direct your responses and give you discernment as to who needs a special touch (a hug, an encouragement, time afterwards, etc.).

Remember, as the leader of the discussion, you are simply a channel God is using to stimulate and guide the conversation--the Holy Spirit is always the teacher. Do *not* do all the talking, but involve every member of the group, always seeing that the sharing is edifying and pointed towards Jesus.

Familiarize yourself with the Prayer Journal on page 355 of the *Faith in the Night Seasons* textbook. Whenever the Lord exposes an area that should be dealt with, be sure to lead the student here. The Inner Court Ritual on page 360 will help them deal with the issue. This section will also provide more information about the questions.

You might also want to become acquainted with pages 369-370 in the *Faith in the Night Seasons* textbook. Here you will find a list of all the Scriptures in the Bible that talk about or mention *night seasons*.

Also, discover the Endnote Section on pages 327-350 in the *Faith in the Night Seasons* textbook . You will find almost 650 endnotes containing hundreds of Scriptural references, other referrals, explanations, bibliography references (other than formal Bibliography on page 371) and amplification of text.

Leading the Study

Always begin the study on time. If everyone realizes that you are punctual, the members of the group will make a greater effort to be there on time--they won't want to miss anything.

At the beginning of your first meeting, you might share that these studies are designed to be discussions, not lectures. Encourage everyone to participate.

The discussion questions in the workbook are designed to be used just as they are written. If you wish, you may read each one aloud to the group. Or you may prefer to express them in your own words. However, unnecessary rewording of the questions is not recommended.

Don't be afraid of silence. People in the group need time to think before responding.

Try to avoid answering your own questions. If necessary, keep rephrasing a question until it is clearly understood. If the group thinks you will always answer for them, they will keep silent.

Encourage more than one answer to each question. You might ask, "What do the rest of you think?" or "Anyone else?" Allow several people to respond.

Never reject an answer. Be as affirming as possible. If a person's answer is clearly wrong, you might ask, "What led you to that conclusion?" Or let the group handle the problem by asking them what they think about the question.

Avoid going off on tangents. If people wander off course, gently bring them back to the question at hand.

Try to end on time. This is often difficult to do, but if you control the pace of the discussion by not spending too much time on some questions, you should be able to finish at the appropriate time. A discussion group of about 45 minutes to an hour is perfect.

Additional Suggestions for Leaders

Besides being that open and cleansed vessel and constantly praying, there are several other *skills* that you, as the leader of the discussion, should pray about developing:

Pray for and develop *good communication skills*. Communication will not only be your words, but also your "body language." Even though someone might share something shocking in the discussion, be careful not to offend the participant by your response. Acknowledge the person, all the while asking God for *His* response to what they have just shared. Be confident that God will give you the Love you need and also the Wisdom you need to respond "wisely in Love."

Try to really understand what the participant is sharing. If necessary, repeat what you think he/she is saying. For example, you might ask: "Is this what you are saying...?" or, "You mean...?"

Another very important asset for you to acquire, as the leader of the group, is to be a *good listener*. Everyone is desperate for someone to listen to them, especially when they are going through critical emotional issues. Whenever someone is talking, give them your undivided attention. Your eyes should be on the person sharing and you should try to acknowledge them as much as you can (again, always praying silently to God for *His* response).

Another vital skill to develop is to *be an encourager*. Set an example for your group by encouraging the members continually. Without encouragement, your sharing times will be nothing more than answering homework questions at school. (You might even suggest that the following week, each of the members of the group phone and encourage someone else in the group.)

One of the most difficult tasks that you will face is *how to keep one person from dominating* the group. You need to allow each person in the group an opportunity to share, but you must prevent any *one* person from doing all the talking (including yourself). One member of the group who continually dominates the discussion can derail and quench an otherwise anointed sharing time. You mustn't rush the person speaking, giving the Holy Spirit ample time to minister and guide the discussion, but at the same time you are responsible to keep the discussion on target and to accomplish all that needs to be done.

A few suggestions to prevent one person from dominating the discussion:

- You might interrupt the particular person speaking and restate what you have just heard him/her say.

- You might repeat the question you previously asked the group. The dominating person might be startled at first by the interruption, but should respond by answering the second question more directly.

- If this does not work, then you should ask the participant to please let the other group members share their views also.

Another invaluable skill for you to have, as the leader of the discussion, is knowing how to *involve all the members* of the group in the discussion. Discussion groups are not for lecturing--each individual must be encouraged to interact. Ideally, everyone should have an opportunity to share. Ask open-ended questions to specific individuals, especially ones that are reluctant to volunteer anything themselves.

Again, it's important not to criticize, make fun of or put anyone down. Remember, be an encourager. Learn how to correct a group member's answer in a positive way and then, as tactfully as you can, go on to the next person.

Helpful Hints for Leaders

Always open the discussion with prayer and close the session with prayer. Pray that God will help each of you to apply the Biblical principles daily.

Start out the first session by sharing a little about yourself. How has *Faith in the Night Seasons* affected or changed your life? Go around the circle and have each member share five minutes about him/herself.

In the succeeding meetings, begin each session by asking:

- "Which key points stood out to you during this session?"

- "Which points challenged you or encouraged you?"

- "Could any of you relate to some of the situations or struggles that were shared in this chapter?

- "Are any of you experiencing similar situations?"

- "In what areas of your life might you be able to apply this teaching?"

Suggest that each member of the group during the week write down any questions they may have while reading the textbook, so they can talk about them during the group discussion.

Reproduce **Charts A-E** in the *Faith in the Night Seasons* textbook and post them in each of the appropriate sessions, so that the group can constantly refer to them.

Finally, stress complete confidentiality. Set an example for the group by being the first to be trustworthy.

Personal Notes